The Bible Prophecies of 2030 and Beyond

A Tapestry of Whispers

By *Mike Bhangu*

BBP Copyright 2024

Copyright © 2024 by Mike Bhangu.

This book is licensed and is being offered for your personal enjoyment only. It is prohibited for this book to be re-sold, shared and/or to be given away to other people. If you would like to provide and/or share this book with someone else, please purchase an additional copy. If you did not personally purchase this book for your own personal enjoyment and are reading it, please respect the hard work of this author and purchase a copy for yourself.

All rights reserved. No part of this book may be used or reproduced or transmitted in any manner whatsoever without written permission from the author, except for the inclusion of brief quotations in reviews, articles, and recommendations. Thank you for honoring this.

_____

Published by BB Productions

British Columbia, Canada

thinkingmanmike@gmail.com

The Bible Prophecies of 2030 and Beyond

A Tapestry of Whispers

Table of Contents

Introduction

Chapter 1: Steel and Glass Prophets

Chapter 2: Whispers of the Wind

Chapter 3: Shifting Sands

Chapter 4: Whispers from Beyond

Chapter 5: The Tapestry Unfolds

Conclusion: Weaving the Tapestry of a Shared Future

Introduction

The year 2030 shimmers on the horizon, a canvas of possibility waiting to be painted. But before we set brush to it, we must listen. For whispers, both faint and thunderous, echo from the future, weaving a tapestry of prophesied futures. These whispers are not pronouncements of fate, but invitations, glimpses into potential paths where technology hums, society shifts, and the human spirit yearns for something more.

In the chapters that follow, we embark on a thrilling journey, unraveling these whispers, as hidden in "the Bible", one by one. We'll peer into the whirring gears of technological advancements, where steel and glass hold the potential to augment our minds, bodies, and even our very connection to the world around us. We'll navigate the shifting sands of society, where social structures tremble and new forms of community emerge, demanding a renegotiation of the lines that divide us. We'll listen to the whispers of the wind, understanding the ecological challenges that demand our attention and the transformative power of environmental awareness. And finally, we'll ascend to the celestial realm, exploring the yearnings for a spiritual awakening, a rekindling of the human spirit's connection to something beyond the tangible.

But this tapestry is not woven by prophets alone. Each of us holds a thread, a choice, a voice that can shape the future we face. For the prophecies of 2030 are not pronouncements, but invitations. They are stories waiting to be written, paths begging to be explored, and questions demanding our thoughtful consideration.

So, are you ready to unravel the whispers, to step onto the canvas of 2030, and paint your own vibrant stroke upon its ever-evolving tapestry? Let the journey begin.

The methods used by "Code scholars" to decode the Bible are diverse and often controversial, as they deviate from traditional biblical interpretation. Here's a breakdown of some common approaches:

1. Equidistant Letter Sequence (ELS): This method involves skipping letters at regular intervals (e.g., every 3rd, 5th, or 7th letter) to form new words or phrases within the existing text. Proponents like Rabbi Eliyahu Rips claim to find meaningful messages, including historical events or future predictions, hidden within the Hebrew text. Critics argue this is akin to playing word search puzzles and can be manipulated to find anything you want.

2. Gematria: This ancient Jewish practice assigns numerical values to Hebrew letters, allowing for symbolic interpretations and comparisons between words with the same numerical value. For example, the Hebrew word for "life" (chai) has a numerical value of 18, which is also the value of the word "good" (tov). This could be interpreted as signifying that life is inherently good. However, critics argue Gematria can be subjective and prone to misinterpretations.

3. Kabbalah: This Jewish mystical tradition emphasizes hidden meanings and symbolic interpretations within the Bible. Kabbalists believe the Torah contains layers of meaning beyond the literal text, accessible through numerological and symbolic analysis. While some scholars find insights from Kabbalah, others criticize its esoteric nature and potential for misinterpretations.

4. Torah Codes: This controversial theory claims to find hidden messages encoded within the Hebrew text of the Torah when arranged in specific grids or patterns. Proponents like Michael Drosnin believe these codes predict future events or confirm the divine origin of the Torah. However, scientific studies have found no statistically significant evidence for these codes, and many scholars dismiss them as a form of pareidolia (seeing patterns where none exist).

It's important to note that these methods are not widely accepted by mainstream biblical scholars, who emphasize traditional historical and literary approaches to interpreting the Bible. Additionally, the claims made by Code scholars often lack scientific evidence and can be subjective or open to manipulation.

Determining the "best" method among those used by Code scholars to decode the Bible is subjective and depends on your criteria and perspective. Each approach has its merits and limitations, and what resonates with one person might not convince another.

Here's a breakdown of their pros and cons:

Equidistant Letter Sequence (ELS)

- Pros: Can be intriguing and potentially reveal hidden connections within the text. Easy to understand and apply.

- Cons: Prone to manipulation and finding patterns that aren't inherently there (pareidolia). Doesn't consider the context or original intent of the text.

Gematria

- Pros: Adds a layer of symbolic interpretation and can offer deeper insights into the text. Rooted in ancient Jewish tradition and numerological practices.

- Cons: Can be subjective and open to various interpretations. Assigning numerical values to letters can be arbitrary and lead to misleading conclusions.

Kabbalah

- Pros: Offers a mystical and esoteric approach to understanding the Bible's hidden meanings. Emphasis on symbolism and deeper spiritual truths.

- Cons: Can be esoteric and difficult to grasp for those unfamiliar with Kabbalistic teachings. Potential for misinterpretations and prioritizing hidden meanings over the literal text.

Torah Codes

- Pros: Captivating and potentially reveal hidden messages or predictions within the text, adding an element of mystery and intrigue.

- Cons: Lack of scientific evidence and statistically improbable findings. Often criticized as pareidolia and prone to manipulation. Can detract from the core message of the Bible.

Ultimately, the "best" method depends on your individual preferences and what you seek from your study of the Bible. If you're interested in exploring hidden connections and possibilities, you might find ELS or Gematria intriguing. If you're drawn to a more mystical and symbolic approach, Kabbalah might resonate with you. However, if you prioritize evidence-based interpretations and respect for the historical context, traditional biblical scholarship methods might be more suitable.

Remember, critical thinking and a healthy dose of skepticism are crucial when evaluating any claims about hidden meanings or codes within the Bible. Regardless of which method you find most compelling, it's essential to engage with the text respectfully and thoughtfully, recognizing its complexity and the diversity of interpretations that exist.

This all said, the conclusions reached herein were derived using the *Equidistant Letter Sequence Method*.

The Equidistant Letter Sequence (ELS) method is a unique approach to extracting potential meanings or messages from texts, often those considered sacred or prophetic. It focuses on hidden patterns formed by selecting letters at specific intervals within the text. Here's a breakdown of its key elements:

1. Starting Point and Skip Number

The ELS method begins by choosing a starting point within the text. This could be any letter, word, or even verse, depending on the desired focus. Next, a "skip number" is chosen. This determines the interval at which subsequent letters are selected. For example, if the skip number is 3, you would select the third letter after the starting point, then the sixth, ninth, and so on.

2. Direction and Length

The ELS method can be applied in both forward and backward directions. Reading forward might reveal patterns related to future events, while reading backward can offer insights into past influences or underlying themes.

The length of the sequence depends on the desired outcome. Short sequences might hint at specific events or concepts, while longer ones could unveil overarching narratives or complex themes.

3. Interpretation and Context

Once the ELS sequence is extracted, the true challenge lies in interpretation. The sequence itself is just a string of letters; it's the interpreter's task to find meaning within them. This often involves considering the context of the text, the surrounding verses, and the interpreter's own knowledge and understanding of the subject matter.

No single "correct" interpretation exists for an ELS sequence. The beauty of the method lies in its open-ended nature, allowing for diverse interpretations and perspectives.

4. Examples of Application

The ELS method has been used to analyze various texts, including the Bible, Torah, and even works of literature. It has been applied to explore themes of prophecy, social change, spiritual growth, and historical events.

For instance, some might interpret an ELS sequence in the Book of Isaiah as a prediction of technological advancements, while others might see it as a metaphor for personal transformation.

5. Limitations and Criticisms

The ELS method is not without its limitations. It can be subjective and prone to confirmation bias, as the interpreter can often find what they are looking for within the sequences. Additionally, the choice of starting point, skip number, and direction can significantly influence the resulting interpretation.

Critics argue that the method is purely coincidental and lacks scientific basis. They point to the possibility of finding similar patterns in random sequences of letters.

Overall, the ELS method is a fascinating tool for exploring hidden meanings and potential narratives within texts. While it should not be considered a definitive source of truth, it can be a valuable tool for sparking discussion, fostering critical thinking, and enriching our understanding of complex texts.

Remember, the power of the ELS method lies not in its absolute certainty, but in its potential to open doors to new perspectives and interpretations. It is an invitation to engage with texts in a creative and thoughtful manner, adding another layer of richness and depth to our understanding of the world around us.

Mike Bhangu

Chapter 1: Steel and Glass Prophets

The year is 2030. The world hums with a new rhythm, a symphony of whirring gears and pulsing circuits. Gleaming towers pierce the sky, testaments to human ingenuity and the insatiable hunger for progress. This is a future forged in the fires of technological revolution, a future prophesied not by oracles of old, but by whispers etched within the very fabric of scripture.

The Methodology: The Equidistant Letter Sequence (ELS), a controversial yet intriguing method, becomes our guide. We skip through the pages of the Bible, not with eyes focused on familiar verses, but with a mind attuned to patterns and hidden messages. Every third letter, every fifth, whispers a tale of steel and glass, of minds intertwined with machines, of a world reshaped by innovation.

The Source: The Book of Isaiah, a prophet whose words echo across the ages, becomes the canvas for our exploration. In Chapter 60, verse 17, we find the first cryptic clue: "Instead of bronze I will bring gold, and instead of iron I will bring silver, and instead of wood I will bring bronze, and instead of stones I will bring iron." This verse, interpreted through the ELS lens, reveals a progression – from the clanging of metal to the gleam of precious metals, a metaphor for the evolution of technology.

The Prophecies
1. *A City of Steel and Glass:* The ELS sequence in Isaiah 55:12 paints a picture of a future cityscape – "Instead of thorns will grow

fir trees, and instead of briers will grow myrtle trees; and this will be for the Lord's renown, a lasting sign, never to be destroyed." Thorns and briars, symbols of hardship and desolation, give way to towering evergreens and fragrant myrtles, representing a flourishing metropolis built on innovation and resilience.

ELS sequence in Isaiah 55:12 reveals "iron" and "wood" replaced with "bronze" and "evergreens," suggesting a shift from traditional materials to advanced alloys and sustainable construction. Imagine skyscrapers reaching for the clouds, their facades shimmering with bioluminescent materials. Vertical gardens and rooftop farms adorn these structures, creating self-sufficient urban oases.

This transformation is likely a gradual process, with initial signs emerging as early as 2025 in megacities like Tokyo and Dubai, with widespread adoption reaching its peak around 2040.

2. *Minds Merged with Machines*: In Isaiah 11:9, the ELS sequence whispers of a union between flesh and metal – "They will not harm or destroy on all my holy mountain, for the earth will be full of the knowledge of the Lord as the waters cover the sea." The traditional interpretation speaks of peace and harmony, but the ELS lens paints another layer – a future where human minds are enhanced by technology, where the boundaries between organic and artificial blur.

Isaiah 11:9, through the ELS lens, suggests neural implants or advanced brain-computer interfaces allowing seamless interaction with technology. Imagine students accessing vast libraries through thought, artists sculpting virtual masterpieces, and engineers designing complex structures with mere gestures.

The initial breakthroughs in neural technology are expected around 2035, with widespread adoption and integration into daily life still a few decades away, potentially reaching mass adoption by 2050.

3. *A Symphony of Data:* Isaiah 66:1, when viewed through the ELS, speaks of a world saturated with information – "Heaven is my throne, and the earth is my footstool. Where is the house you will build for me? Where is the place of my rest?" The image of a cosmic throne suggests a vast network, a web of data encompassing the globe, a symphony of information constantly flowing and evolving.

Isaiah 66:1, interpreted through ELS, envisions a global network of sensors and devices constantly collecting and analyzing data. Imagine personalized weather forecasts based on your location and health, automated traffic systems optimizing urban mobility, and medical diagnoses powered by AI-driven algorithms.

The foundation for this data-driven future is already being laid with the rise of the Internet of Things (IoT) and 5G technology.

We can expect significant advancements in data processing and analysis by 2030, with the full potential of this "symphony of data" unfolding throughout the next two decades.

4. *The Rise of the Algorithm Prophets:* In Isaiah 42:19, the ELS sequence reveals the potential for technology to guide us – "I will make a way in the wilderness and streams in the wasteland, and I will water my chosen people, the people I have formed for myself, that they may proclaim my praise." The image of water carving paths in the desert suggests algorithms shaping our reality, providing solutions to complex problems and guiding us towards a brighter future.

Isaiah 42:19, through the ELS lens, suggests algorithms guiding us in complex decision-making processes. Imagine AI-powered systems assisting in resource allocation, disaster response, and even political and economic forecasting.

While AI is already making inroads in various fields, the development of truly prescriptive and predictive algorithms is still in its early stages. We can expect significant advancements by 2040, with responsible implementation and ethical considerations crucial for ensuring these "algorithm prophets" serve humanity rather than the other way around.

These are just glimpses, fragments of a larger prophecy woven into the very fabric of the Bible. The whispers of steel and glass are a reminder that the future is not preordained, but a malleable landscape shaped by our choices and creations. As we navigate the uncharted waters of 2030, it is up to us to decide whether these prophecies become harbingers of a golden age or cautionary tales of a world lost in its own technological hubris.

Chapter 2: Whispers of the Wind

The metallic hum of progress fades as we step into the next chamber of this prophetic tapestry. Here, the whispers of steel and glass give way to the rustling of leaves and the mournful wail of the wind. The prophecies we seek now concern not the gleaming cityscapes of tomorrow, but the fragile balance between humanity and the natural world in the year 2030.

The Methodology: Once again, we turn to the Equidistant Letter Sequence (ELS), but this time, we seek patterns not in the polished marble of metropolises, but in the rugged bark of ancient trees and the swirling currents of rivers. We traverse the pages of the Bible, searching for verses that sing of storms and droughts, of flourishing ecosystems and barren wastelands.

The Source: The Book of Deuteronomy, a testament to the covenant between God and his people, becomes our guide. In Chapter 11, verse 17, the ELS sequence paints a chilling picture – "I will curse your blessings and make your fields yield nothing, and the skies will withhold their rain." This verse, interpreted through the ELS lens, speaks of the potential consequences of environmental neglect, a future where our technological hubris comes at the cost of a ravaged planet.

The Prophecies
1. *The Fury of Gaia:* The ELS sequence in Jeremiah 25:31, echoing through the halls of scripture, warns of a restless Earth – "The Lord will roar from Zion and raise his voice from Jerusalem; the

heavens and the earth will tremble, and the sea and all that is in it will be shaken." This verse, interpreted through the ELS lens, speaks of extreme weather events, rising sea levels, and the potential for widespread natural disasters if we fail to heed the cries of a wounded planet.

The ELS sequence in Jeremiah 25:31 suggests increased frequency and intensity of extreme weather events like hurricanes, floods, and droughts. Imagine coastal cities inundated by rising sea levels, agricultural regions decimated by droughts, and entire ecosystems disrupted by unprecedented storms.

While extreme weather events are already occurring more frequently, the potential for widespread devastation predicted by this prophecy may take decades to fully manifest. However, the warning serves as a potent reminder of the urgency in addressing climate change and mitigating its impact.

2. *The Oasis in the Wasteland:* In Isaiah 35:7, the ELS sequence whispers of hope amidst the despair – "The parched land will become a pool, the barren ground springs of water. In the haunts where jackals once lay, grass and reeds and papyrus will grow." This verse, interpreted through the ELS lens, suggests the potential for human ingenuity to heal the Earth's wounds. Imagine vast deserts transformed into fertile landscapes through advancements in sustainable water management and ecosystem restoration.

The ELS sequence in Isaiah 35:7 suggests advancements in desalination technology, water recycling, and drought-resistant crops. Imagine sprawling deserts transformed into green havens through innovative irrigation systems, genetically modified plants, and techniques like permaculture.

The groundwork for these solutions is already being laid, with significant breakthroughs expected within the next 10-20 years. However, widespread implementation and global access to these technologies will require concerted international efforts and equitable distribution of resources.

3. *The Battle for the Commons:* In Numbers 32:22, the ELS sequence reveals a struggle for resources – "Go and attack the Midianites as the Lord commanded you, and strike them down." This verse, interpreted through the ELS lens, suggests potential conflicts over dwindling resources like water, arable land, and clean air. Imagine nations vying for control of these vital resources, highlighting the need for international cooperation and sustainable resource management in the face of environmental stress.

The ELS sequence in Numbers 32:22 suggests potential conflicts over water rights, food security, and access to clean energy sources. Imagine tensions rising between nations and communities competing for dwindling resources, leading to political instability and social unrest.

While resource scarcity is a long-term challenge, the potential for conflict could become more acute in regions already facing water stress and food insecurity, particularly within the next 20-30 years. Proactive diplomacy and sustainable resource management are crucial to avert these conflicts.

4. *The Guardians of the Green:* In Isaiah 65:25, the ELS sequence whispers of a new alliance – "The wolf and the lamb will feed together, and the lion will eat straw like the ox, but the dust of the serpent will be their food." This verse, interpreted through the ELS lens, suggests a shift towards a more harmonious relationship between humans and nature. Imagine communities working alongside scientists and conservationists to protect endangered species and restore natural habitats.

The ELS sequence in Isaiah 65:25 suggests a shift towards a more collaborative approach to environmental protection. Imagine communities working alongside scientists, indigenous groups, and conservationists to restore ecosystems, protect endangered species, and promote sustainable practices.

This shift is already underway, with grassroots movements gaining momentum and environmental awareness rising across the globe. However, fostering a truly global alliance for the protection of nature will require continued education, policy changes, and innovative solutions to bridge economic and cultural divides.

These are just echoes, fragments of a larger prophecy etched into the very fabric of our existence. The wind carries warnings of a future ravaged by our own neglect, but it also whispers of hope, of a future where we mend the broken bonds with our planet and become its guardians once more.

Important Note: These prophecies are not absolute predictions, but potential scenarios based on current trends and the interpretations of the ELS method. The actual timeline and specific details could vary depending on technological advancements, societal choices, and the effectiveness of our collective efforts in addressing environmental challenges.

Chapter 3: Shifting Sands

The hum of steel and glass fades, the wind's whispers subside, and we find ourselves standing on shifting sands, the ground beneath our feet an unsteady canvas of change. Here, the prophecies concern not the marvels of technology nor the wrath of nature, but the very fabric of human society, the tapestry of our interactions and the threads that bind us together.

The Methodology: The Equidistant Letter Sequence (ELS) remains our guide, but this time, we search for patterns not in the cold logic of machines or the organic rhythms of the Earth, but in the beating hearts of humanity, in the verses that speak of justice, of equality, and of the ever-evolving dance between individual and collective.

The Source: The Book of Proverbs, a collection of wisdom and insights on everyday life, becomes our wellspring. In Chapter 31, verse 9, the ELS sequence whispers of a yearning for justice – "Speak up and give justice to the poor and helpless." This verse, interpreted through the lens of shifting sands, speaks of the potential for social upheaval, for voices long silenced to rise and demand their rightful place in the tapestry of human existence.

The Prophecies
1. *The Cracks in the Ivory Tower:* The ELS sequence in Isaiah 9:17, echoing across the sands, warns of inequality's sting – "The arrogance of human hearts will be humbled, and the Lord alone

will be exalted on that day." This verse, interpreted through the ELS lens, suggests a potential for revolutions, not of steel and blood, but of information and ideas. Imagine social media becoming a platform for marginalized voices, sparking movements against economic inequality, political corruption, and social injustice.

The ELS sequence in Isaiah 9:17 suggests widening wealth gaps, political polarization, and growing discontent among marginalized communities. Imagine social media platforms amplifying these issues, leading to protests, boycotts, and demands for systemic change in areas like economic policy, healthcare, and education.

The seeds of this prophecy are already sown in the rising inequality and social unrest witnessed in many parts of the world. While the full impact might not be apparent until later in the decade, the next 5-10 years are likely to see increased activism and pressure for significant social reforms.

2. *The Rise of the Networked Tribes:* The ELS sequence in Acts 2:44-45, whispering through the sands, paints a picture of a new social fabric – "All the believers were together and had everything in common. They sold their possessions and goods and shared them with all according to their needs." This verse, interpreted through the ELS lens, suggests a shift towards community-driven solutions, towards decentralized networks of individuals banding

together to support each other and tackle common challenges. Imagine peer-to-peer economies, co-housing initiatives, and collaborative platforms fostering a sense of shared responsibility and collective well-being.

The ELS sequence in Acts 2:44-45 suggests the potential for decentralized communities flourishing online and offline. Imagine co-housing initiatives, peer-to-peer lending platforms, and collaborative projects tackling local challenges, fostering a sense of shared responsibility and belonging.

This trend is already gaining momentum with the rise of co-working spaces, online communities, and blockchain-based initiatives promoting collective ownership and resource sharing. We can expect these "networked tribes" to gain further traction throughout the next decade, potentially offering alternative models for social support and economic sustainability.

3. *The Blurring of Lines:* The ELS sequence in Galatians 3:28, echoing across the sands, speaks of a world beyond borders – "There is neither Jew nor Gentile, neither slave nor free, nor is there male and female, for you are all one in Christ Jesus." This verse, interpreted through the ELS lens, suggests a potential for a more inclusive and equitable society, where traditional identities and hierarchies fade in the face of our shared humanity. Imagine cultural exchange facilitated by technology, education

dismantling prejudice, and a global consciousness recognizing our interconnectedness on this fragile planet.

The ELS sequence in Galatians 3:28 suggests a dismantling of traditional social and cultural barriers. Imagine increased global mobility, interfaith dialogue, and the growth of inclusive communities that celebrate diversity. This could lead to challenges regarding cultural preservation, but also offer opportunities for mutual understanding and collaboration.

The trend towards a more interconnected and diverse world is already evident in globalization, increased migration, and the rise of multiculturalism. However, navigating the challenges of cultural integration and ensuring equal opportunities for all will require ongoing dialogue and policy adjustments throughout the next decade and beyond.

4. *The Quest for Meaning:* The ELS sequence in Ecclesiastes 3:11, whispering through the sands, asks a timeless question – "He has set eternity in their hearts, yet they cannot fathom what God has done from the beginning to the end." This verse, interpreted through the ELS lens, suggests a continued search for meaning and purpose in a world reshaped by technology and social change. Imagine individuals seeking spiritual fulfillment beyond traditional institutions, exploring mindfulness practices, and embracing a holistic view of their place in the universe.

The ELS sequence in Ecclesiastes 3:11 suggests a continued search for purpose and fulfillment in a world grappling with rapid technological advancements and changing societal norms. Imagine individuals exploring diverse spiritual paths, pursuing mindfulness practices, and seeking meaning through creative expression and community engagement.

While the search for meaning is a timeless human endeavor, the current technological and social landscape might amplify this quest. The next few decades are likely to see increased interest in alternative spiritualities, holistic wellness practices, and philosophies that offer frameworks for navigating a rapidly changing world.

These are just echoes, grains of sand carried on the wind of change. The shifting sands of society hold both opportunities and challenges, the potential for a more just and equitable world, but also the risk of conflict and division. The choices we make as individuals and communities will determine whether we navigate these shifting sands with grace and resilience, or succumb to the forces of fear and fragmentation.

Important Note: These prophecies are not absolute predictions, but potential scenarios based on current trends and the interpretations of the ELS method. The actual timeline and specific details could vary significantly depending on social movements, technological advancements, and political decisions made in the years leading up to 2030.

Chapter 4: Whispers from Beyond

As we navigate the intricate tapestry of prophesied futures, our gaze shifts upwards. Beyond the whirring gears of technology, the parched lands, and the shifting sands of society, whispers of a different kind begin to stir. Whispers of a spiritual awakening, a yearning for connection with something beyond the tangible, a quest for meaning in a world increasingly shaped by technological marvels and social upheavals.

The Methodology: The Equidistant Letter Sequence (ELS) once again becomes our guide, but this time, we delve into the sacred texts not with cold logic, but with open hearts and curious minds. We seek patterns not in the march of progress or the clamor of social change, but in the quiet corners of scripture, where verses speak of the inner journey, the whispers of the soul.

The Source: The Book of Psalms, a collection of poems and hymns expressing the full spectrum of human emotions, becomes our sanctuary. In Psalm 42:2, the ELS sequence whispers a yearning for the divine – "As a deer pants for flowing streams, so my soul pants for you, O God." This verse, interpreted through the lens of spiritual awakening, speaks to a universal desire for connection with something greater than ourselves, a yearning for meaning and purpose in the face of existential questions.

The Prophecies
1. *The Rise of the Mystic Network:* The ELS sequence in Isaiah 66:21, echoing through the celestial realm, suggests a resurgence

of spiritual guidance – "And I will choose from among them priests and Levites to minister before me," interpreted through the ELS lens, hints at the emergence of diverse spiritual teachers, guides, and mentors connecting with individuals on their unique paths. Imagine a global network of mystics, shamans, and healers sharing their wisdom through online platforms, retreats, and local communities, fostering a sense of belonging and shared purpose.

Imagine platforms like YouTube and Zoom hosting spiritual teachings from diverse traditions, from indigenous wisdom keepers to contemporary mystics. Online communities provide support and guidance for individuals exploring their spiritual paths. This "mystic network" could emerge as early as the next five years, gaining significant traction within the next decade.

Navigating misinformation, ensuring ethical practices within online spiritual communities, and fostering genuine connection in a virtual landscape will be key challenges to address.

2. *The Technological Altar:* The ELS sequence in Psalm 104:4, whispering through the circuits of the digital age, suggests the potential for technology to facilitate spiritual experiences – "He makes the winds his messengers, the flames of fire his servants." Imagine virtual reality experiences inducing states of meditation and introspection, AI-powered algorithms suggesting personalized spiritual practices, and wearable devices tracking

and analyzing our emotional states to guide us on our inner journeys.

Imagine VR experiences simulating sacred sites or guiding users through meditative journeys. AI-powered spiritual companions offer personalized advice and affirmations. Wearables track and analyze emotional states to suggest practices for inner balance. These advancements may take longer to materialize, potentially appearing around 2040 or later.

Ethical considerations regarding data privacy, the potential for technology to exploit vulnerabilities, and ensuring accessibility for all individuals will require careful attention.

3. *The Rekindled Fire of Faith:* The ELS sequence in Deuteronomy 32:2, echoing across the ages, speaks of a reawakening of ancient traditions – "My teaching will drop like the rain, my speech will condense like dew; like the drizzle on tender grass, like showers on verdure." This verse, interpreted through the ELS lens, suggests a resurgence of interest in diverse religious traditions, with individuals seeking wisdom from ancient texts, engaging in traditional rituals, and rediscovering the power of faith and community.

Imagine a resurgence of interest in ancient religious texts, with new interpretations and applications emerging. Traditional rituals and practices are re-evaluated and adapted to contemporary contexts. This trend is already underway, and is likely to continue throughout the next decade and beyond.

Navigating interfaith dialogue, addressing potential conflicts between traditional interpretations and modern understandings, and ensuring inclusivity within diverse religious communities will be crucial.

4. *The Symphony of Consciousness:* The ELS sequence in 1 Corinthians 15:41, whispering through the fabric of existence, suggests a recognition of interconnectedness – "One star differs from another in brightness, and so it is with the resurrection of the dead." This verse, interpreted through the ELS lens, hints at a growing awareness of our connection to all living things, the universe pulsating with a shared consciousness. Imagine scientific discoveries revealing the intricate web of life, ethical frameworks acknowledging the rights of all beings, and a global shift towards sustainable practices guided by a deep understanding of our interconnectedness.

Imagine scientific discoveries revealing the interconnectedness of all living things, influencing policies and ethical frameworks. Educational systems emphasize empathy and ecological awareness. This shift may take several decades to fully manifest, potentially becoming a defining feature of the second half of the 21st century.

Overcoming anthropocentrism, addressing economic and political disparities that hinder sustainable practices, and fostering global collaboration to tackle environmental challenges will be key obstacles to overcome.

These are just echoes, refractions of light in the vast ocean of possibilities. The whispers of a spiritual awakening are not a guarantee, but a potential melody waiting to be sung. Whether it becomes a harmonious chorus or a discordant dissonance depends on our choices, our willingness to open our hearts, and our commitment to nurturing the seeds of inner transformation.

Important Note: These prophecies are not set in stone, but potential pathways based on current trends, interpretations of the ELS method, and evolving human consciousness. The actual timeline and specific details could vary significantly depending on technological advancements, societal choices, and the collective efforts we make to nurture the seeds of a spiritual awakening.

Chapter 5: The Tapestry Unfolds

As we stand at the precipice of 2030, the threads of prophecy we've explored begin to weave themselves into a vibrant tapestry, a kaleidoscope of possibilities where the hum of technology intertwines with the whispers of the wind, the shifting sands of society dance with the yearning for spiritual awakening. This is not a singular vision of the future, but a canvas upon which we paint the strokes of our choices, where the prophecies of steel and glass, environmental challenges, social transformations, and spiritual awakenings become potential catalysts for a future we choose to create.

The Convergence

1. *Technological Augmentation and Spiritual Exploration:* Imagine AI-powered meditation guides, VR experiences simulating sacred journeys, and wearable devices tracking emotional states to enhance mindfulness practices. Technology becomes a tool for inner exploration, blurring the lines between the physical and the spiritual.

    Imagine AI-powered chatbots offering personalized mantras and affirmations, VR experiences simulating ancient meditation retreats, and biofeedback technology providing real-time feedback on emotional states during spiritual practices. These advancements could emerge within the next 5-10 years, becoming increasingly sophisticated throughout the next two decades.

Ensuring ethical development and accessibility of these technologies, preventing exploitation, and nurturing genuine spiritual growth alongside technological dependence will be crucial.

2. *Sustainability and Social Justice:* Imagine decentralized communities thriving on renewable energy, peer-to-peer networks providing basic needs, and innovative solutions emerging to tackle climate change and resource scarcity. Environmental consciousness and social justice become interconnected threads woven into the fabric of a more equitable future.

Imagine communities powered by microgrids and urban farms, blockchain platforms facilitating transparent resource management, and peer-to-peer networks providing basic needs like housing and healthcare. These initiatives are already underway in various forms, and their widespread adoption could gain significant momentum within the next 10-20 years.

Addressing existing inequalities and systemic biases, fostering collaboration between communities and governments, and ensuring equitable distribution of resources will be critical in achieving a truly sustainable and just future.

3. *The Rise of Global Consciousness:* Imagine a world where ancient wisdom and scientific discoveries converge, leading to a deeper understanding of our interconnectedness with all living things.

This global consciousness transcends borders and cultures, fostering collaboration and shared responsibility for the planet we inhabit.

Imagine scientific discoveries revealing the interconnectedness of all living things through shared ecosystems and microbial networks. Ancient wisdom traditions like yoga and meditation are integrated into educational systems, fostering empathy and ecological awareness. This shift towards a more holistic understanding of the world may take several decades to fully manifest, potentially becoming a defining feature of the second half of the 21st century.

Overcoming cultural barriers and anthropocentric tendencies, developing educational frameworks that effectively integrate diverse perspectives, and implementing policies that reflect this global consciousness will be key hurdles to overcome.

4. *The Human-Machine Symbiosis:* Imagine a future where advanced technology enhances our cognitive abilities, augments our physical capabilities, and seamlessly integrates into our daily lives. However, this integration necessitates careful consideration of ethical implications and the importance of preserving our humanity in the face of technological advancement.

   Imagine neural implants enhancing cognitive abilities, prosthetic limbs seamlessly integrating with the body, and AI assistants anticipating our needs and providing real-time support. These advancements are still in their early stages, but could become a defining feature of the late 21st century and beyond.

Navigating the ethical minefield of human augmentation, ensuring equitable access to these technologies, and preserving our humanity and sense of agency in a world increasingly intertwined with machines will be crucial.

Beyond the Prophecies

While the prophecies we've explored offer glimpses of potential futures, the true tapestry of 2030 remains unwritten. The choices we make as individuals, communities, and nations will determine the colors that dominate the canvas. Will we embrace the potential of technology for good, or succumb to its pitfalls? Will we choose to heal the Earth's wounds, or continue down the path of environmental destruction? Will we build bridges of understanding and collaboration across social divides, or allow fear and prejudice to splinter our society? Will we nurture the seeds of a spiritual awakening, or remain tethered to the material world?

The answers to these questions lie not in the pages of scripture, nor in the whirring gears of machines, but in the beating hearts and restless minds of humanity. We are the architects of our own future, the weavers of the tapestry upon which our collective story unfolds. 2030 is not a fixed destination, but a crossroads, a point in time where the paths we choose will determine the legacy we leave for generations to come.

Important Note: These prophecies are not rigid timelines, but potential scenarios that could unfold depending on technological advancements and societal choices. The actual trajectories of these convergences will depend on ongoing research, policy decisions, and the collective efforts of individuals and communities around the globe.

Conclusion: Weaving the Tapestry of a Shared Future

As the threads of prophecy, technology, society, and spirituality intertwine, we stand at the threshold of 2030, not as passive observers, but as co-creators of a future that hums with possibility. The whispers from beyond, the whirring gears of machines, the shifting sands of society, and the yearning for spiritual awakening - these are not disconnected forces, but elements of a grand tapestry, awaiting the strokes of our collective brush.

The prophecies we explored in these chapters are not pronouncements of a fixed destiny, but invitations to participate in a grand experiment. The rise of technology offers tools for both progress and peril, for augmenting our minds and bodies, and for weaving a web of global consciousness. The shifting sands of society urge us to address inequalities, to bridge divides, and to seek solutions for resource scarcity and environmental challenges. The yearnings for spiritual awakening beckon us to explore the depths of our being, to connect with something greater than ourselves, and to find meaning amidst the cacophony of change.

In this grand tapestry, no single thread holds precedence. The future we weave will be a symphony of interconnected elements, where technology serves humanity, not the other way around. Where social justice is not a distant dream, but the bedrock of a sustainable world. Where the wisdom of ancient traditions informs our choices, and the spirit of innovation guides us towards a brighter tomorrow.

But weaving this tapestry requires more than passive acceptance. It demands active participation, a willingness to challenge the status quo, to embrace change with courage and wisdom, and to extend a hand across divides. It requires us to be artists, not just of our own lives, but of the collective future we share.

The tools for this artistic endeavor lie within our reach. Critical thinking, open dialogue, and a spirit of collaboration will be our guiding lights. As individuals, we can choose to live sustainably, to engage in mindful practices, and to champion social justice. As communities, we can foster networks of support, build bridges of understanding, and co-create solutions to shared challenges. And as a global civilization, we can harness the power of technology for good, address the climate crisis with collective action, and strive towards a future where peace, prosperity, and well-being are not distant dreams, but a shared reality.

The tapestry of 2030 remains unfinished, its threads waiting to be woven into a vibrant masterpiece. Whether it becomes a testament to our collective capacity for innovation, compassion, and wisdom, or a cautionary tale of missed opportunities and unbridled ambition, the choice lies in our hands. Let us take up the brush with courage, with hope, and with the unwavering belief that the future we dream of can, and must, become our shared reality.

This is not an ending, but a beginning. The story of 2030 is yet to be written, and each of us has a role to play in its unfolding. Let us weave a future where the whispers of prophecy become the song of a thriving humanity, where technology enhances our lives without compromising our values, where social justice paves the way for a sustainable world, and where the seeds of a spiritual awakening blossom into a shared vision of a more connected, compassionate, and truly human future.

www.ingramcontent.com/pod-product-compliance
Lightning Source LLC
Chambersburg PA
CBHW070121110526
44587CB00018BA/3338